GOD ALWAYS DID

akhira

GOD ALWAYS DID

Copyright © 2023 by akhira

independently published

ISBN: 9798865187462

instagram.com/god.always.did
tiktok.com/@god.always.did
instagram.com/dyingful
instagram.com/akhirapoetry
twitter.com/akhirapoetry
tiktok.com/@akhirapoetry

NO ONE BELIEVED IN ME,
BUT I KNOW GOD DID

GOD ALWAYS DID

God has big plans for you.
Believe it.

God will never make you wait
for no reason.

Trust His timing.

God's timing is better than your timing

God knows when is the best time
to answer your prayers.

if your heart is in a rush, remind yourself,
"beautiful things take time."

one day you'll be at the place
you always wanted to be.

You're about to walk into one of
the best chapters of your life.

Get ready for it.

what was meant for you
will always be yours

stop worrying and start praying.
God can change everything

God says, stay patient.

My timing is perfect.
I have something bigger planned
for you and trust Me…

you'll love it.

God knows when you are ready for it
have faith in His timing.

just wait until the right one comes along.
God is going to blow your mind with
a love that you never knew existed

for all the hard things you are going
through lately, here's a little remind
that you are doing your best and
you are going to get through it

not everything in life will go according
to your plan, and that's OK

God knows the right time
the right place, the right person
and the right answer to your prayers

by the end of this year
everything will be much better
things will be better
you will be happier

very soon you will smile and say
God, this is more than i prayed for

one day, you'll be living the life
you prayed for

if it's God's will, it will happen
if it's not, He has a better plan

a small talk with God can actually fix a lot

you've asked God for peace
so don't be surprised when
He starts removing things
and people from your life

focus on you.
you've done enough for everyone else.

in God's perfect timing
everything will turn out right

God will make a way.
He did it before.
He will do it again.

Have faith.

believe in sudden positive shifts.
things can change for you at any time.
trust that.

get comfortable with waiting
a little longer for the things
you deserve

that rejection was God's redirection

you are about to receive a blessing
that you've been waiting for

God is reminding you that
He will never leave your side

if you have the chance to make
people happy, just do it.

sometimes people are struggling
silently. maybe your act of kindness
can make their day.

so many doors will open when you
realize that it's okay to start over.

remember that.

God is bigger than whatever
is stressing you out.

God is going to REPLACE everything
you lost with something way better

stop looking for a partner.
focus on growing yourself
and the right person will
eventually find you

God, i'm tired, but i trust You.

what you've been praying
about is on the way.

you are going to be at the right place
at the right time for what's meant to be

you deserve someone who has plans
on marrying you one day

you will get better maybe not today
but someday

you will soon be healed
and everything will be okay

just when you are about to lose all hope
God sends you a big blessing to remind you
that you have been heard

although things may be hard today.
tt will get better tomorrow.

have faith that God will bring you through.

may you soon meet the reason why
God did not allow you to settle.

whatever you do in life just make sure
at the end of the day you are happy

life is way too short for stress
and unhappiness

unfortunately life doesn't wait for you to be okay, get up, pray, and keep going.

be proud of yourself
at least you are trying

may the last months of 2023
be the plot twist you've been
waiting for

i don't really say it enough
but thank you God for carrying me
through my worst days and my best days

at the end of the day
it's only God
who keeps His promise

always remind yourself that you are blessed
in so many ways already

there is no need to rush

what's meant for you
always arrives right on time

when love comes your way again

may it be God sent, safe, secure, reassuring
and lead to marriage

God wants to remind you that
His timing is perfect
stop worrying, stop stressing
God is moving mountains

learn to live when people leave

never go back to someone
who chose someone else over you

don't do that to yourself

have some faith, it's going to be okay

don't worry too much
God will provide

always remember that

God's plan is always worth the wait

God will open the right doors for you

God knows you're tired.
pray, wait, trust.

God is reminding you that
He has a plan for your life
that is better than your plan

you never know when
God is going to bless you

good things happen when you
least expect them to.

i pray that God will bless you
before this month is over

stay single until you meet
someone who shows you
how important you really are

you are already blessed
in so many ways, focus on that

i am at peace with God's plans and timing
what's for me will be for me

God heard you, just be patient

have faith, God already
prepared the best answer

God does not forget your prayers
He answers when the time is right.

sometimes a delay in your plan
is God's protection

trust God with what you have prayed for this year

God has the most amazing plan for you
be patient

trust God's timing
it may not be the timing we want
but it's the timing we need

trust the delay that God allows

one day you'll see why
God made you wait

God is about to open that door
you've been praying for

God knows when you are ready for it
have faith in His timing

don't forget God when you get
what you prayed for

if a broken heart brings you closer to God,
then thank God for it

thank God before
you go to sleep tonight

with God, all things are possible

put God first and you will never be last

have patience, God is not finished yet

God has a plan
trust it
enjoy it
live it

God is going to do something for you that is so unexplainable that your only answer will be *"God did it"*.

sometimes all you can do is leave it
in God's hands and rest

it's different when it's not forced
and it's God's timing

God has planned you for me

i'd rather repeat a prayer one thousand
times than have the devil enjoy my silence

i'm not sure who needs to hear this,
this morning but God removes to replace

you won't have to chase what God sent
and that's how you'll know

God will put you back together right in
front of the very people who broke you

maybe God closed that door because
He knew you were worth so much more

if God is all you have,
you have all you need

i pray not because i need something,
but because i have a lot to thank God for

God knows WHEN
to send you EXACTLY
what you need

when you don't know
what to do,
PRAY.

i talk to God about you

my day is better
when i talk to God first

i want what God wants for me

you never lose when
trusting God

it's never luck… it's always God

my heart is at peace because
i know God is working

God is going to give you
the strength to get through this

God is always with you

God's plan > my plan

pray. wait. trust.

go to God first, not last

my real "*glow up*" was when
i began to focus on God

stress happens when you forget
God is in charge

i know God is the only reason
i have made it this far

i didn't get lucky
i prayed
a lot

God knows when it's time
for you to be seen

if you prayed about it
then there is no reason
to worry, when the time
is right, God will give you
what is yours

please God, not people

the devil wants us to worry,
God wants us to pray

God's "*no*" is not a rejection
it's a redirection

pray about it as much as you think about it

find peace in knowing God
will always lead you to
where you need to be

you are beautiful just the way
God made you

God knows
the when
the where
the why
and the how.
show up.
do your part.
then let go
and trust
Him to do
the rest

God is going to make a way
keep praying

the cure to a lonely heart
is to be alone with God

when you don't know what to do,
pray.

just wait and see
why God had you wait
what God is doing is
beyond what you could
ever pray or think of

God is saying to you today
"if you saw what i was sending you
you wouldn't mind waiting. get ready"

a lot can happen in a month,
trust God

notice how God is looking out for you
in the little ways too

God is fixing the situation
you are stressing about

God, i'm thanking you
even before it happens

one day you will realize that God
was putting it all together the whole time

peace comes when you pray

remember that God will always
know what your silent heart wants

God's timing, not mine
God's will, not mine
God's plan, not mine
God's glory, not mine

nobody can stop what God
is about to do in your life

God has already prepared the way
He is just preparing you

God is going to give you more
than you asked for

he prayed for her
she prayed for him
God answered them,
both in His timing.

good days, pray.
bad days, pray.
everyday, pray.

it's going to be a "*God did it*"
kind of year for me

one little prayer can
change one huge situation

God's timing is designed to
teach you to trust

maybe you're in the middle
of what you prayed for

God, i couldn't have made it
this far without You.

thank You.

i've never seen a day that God
didn't come through for me

have you ever cried while praying
because it's really that deep?

you really don't know pain til you sat
and begged God to heal your heart

reasons why i'm not panicking

1. God

start your day off with prayer, you
don't know what it just blocked

ain't nobody but God carrying
me through these days

i have God, i'm good

before 2024 comes,
God will change your story

i pray this world finds God again

praying for you is my love language

God sees. God listens. God
knows. God gives. God cares.

with or without problems
talk to God

that glow hits different when God
turns that pain into peace

pray, then let it go
don't try manipulate
or force the outcome
just trust God
to open
the right doors
at the right time

and suddenly it's your turn and
God makes it all happen for you

pray about it before
you make that **decision**

God removes.
God replaces.
what's coming next
is greater than
what you lost

give it to God
and go to sleep

my future is in God's hand

don't be ashamed to talk about God,
be ashamed not to

if God wants someone in your life
He will find a way to cross your paths
you won't have to make it happen
yourself

i pray for a love story
that brings glory to God

trust God's plan, He knows best

one day you will see why
God made you wait

no one knows how much you
cried that day, but God knows

trust the delays God allows

God's not too slow, we are too impatient

God already knows, stop stressing

when the time is right, God will make it happen

God is preparing you for
what you have been praying for

dear God, thank you for another day

find peace by focusing on
God's promises

dear God,
i'm sorry for the times i'm overwhelmed
and worried about my future that i forget
You are faithful and keep Your promises

i don't know who needs to hear this
but be patient…

God hears your prayers

don't quit, someone is praying for you
God is on your side

don't rush what God is taking time
to prepare, trust His timing

sometimes a delay in your plans
is God's protection

GOD, GOALS, GROWING, & GLOWING

one day you will have
everything you prayed for

BELIEVE IT

imagine how many times God
has saved you from something
and you had no idea

try again, this time with God

sometimes a heartbreak
can bring you closer to God
than you think

one day you will realize God was
putting it together the whole time

end each day
by thanking God

first it hurts you, then it brings you
closer to God

God, i need you, i can't overcome it alone

God is going to open a better door
than the one you prayed for

God is getting ready to disappoint
everyone who expected you to fail

God has heard your prayer

don't be surprised when
God answers your prayers
be ready

if you are praying for it
God is working on it

everything will work in your favor
just trust God

God.
Thank you for never leaving me.

God is always listening, remember that

God will always be there for you

thank God for everything

before i close my eyes
i pray God forgives me

Made in United States
Troutdale, OR
11/17/2023